AF358616

Chapter 1
Introduction to Mindful Photography

Meet Mounjaro, the curious cat who loves to explore the world around her. She discovers the art of photography and learns that it's not just about taking pictures, but also about being mindful and present in the moment.

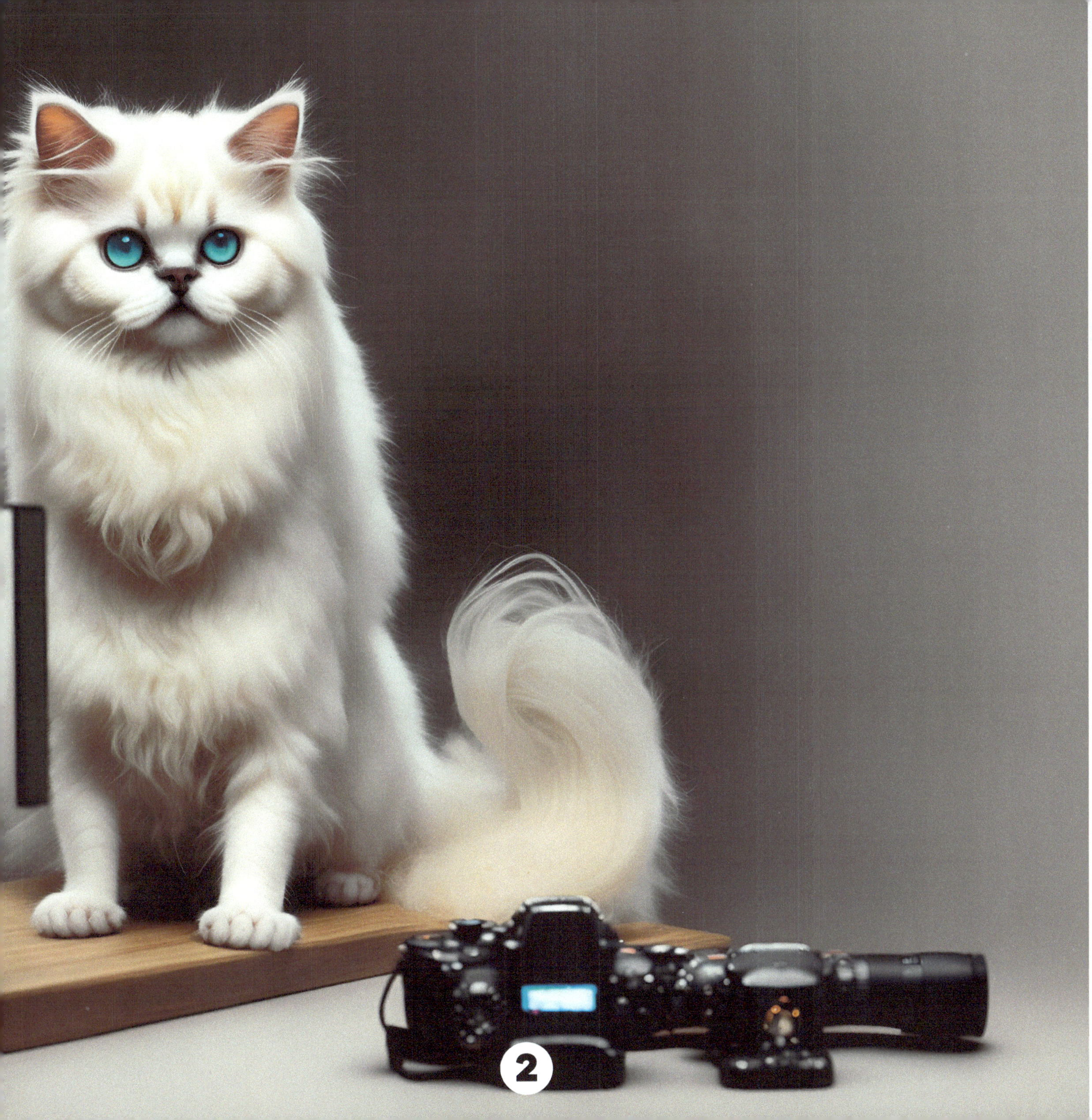

Chapter 2
The Camera and Its Functions

Mounjaro learns about the different parts of the camera and how they work together to create a photograph. She discovers the shutter speed, aperture, ISO, and other camera functions.

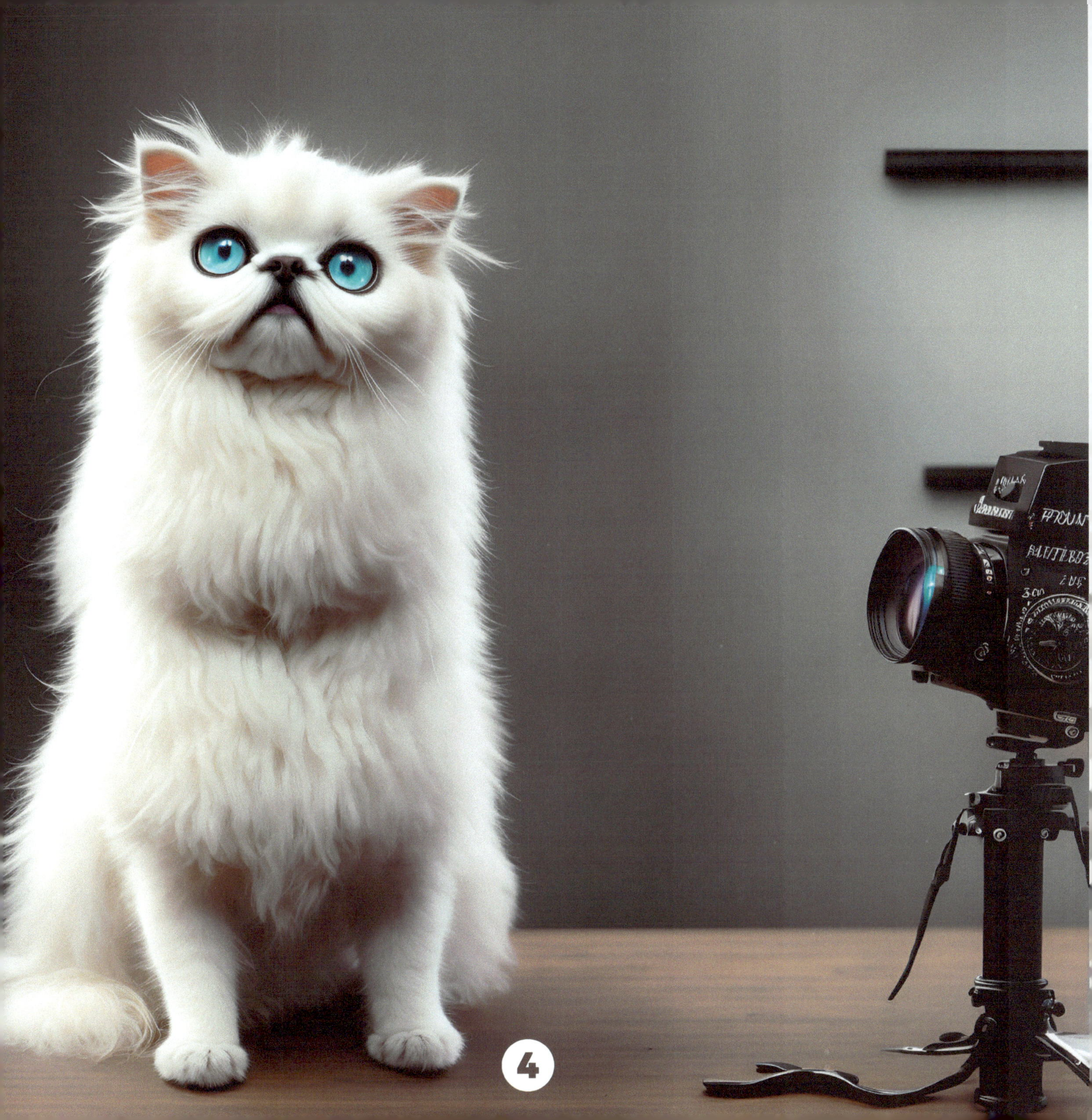

Chapter 3
Light and Shadow

Mounjaro learns that light and shadow can transform a photo and create a mood. She experiments with natural light, artificial light, and shadows to create interesting effects.

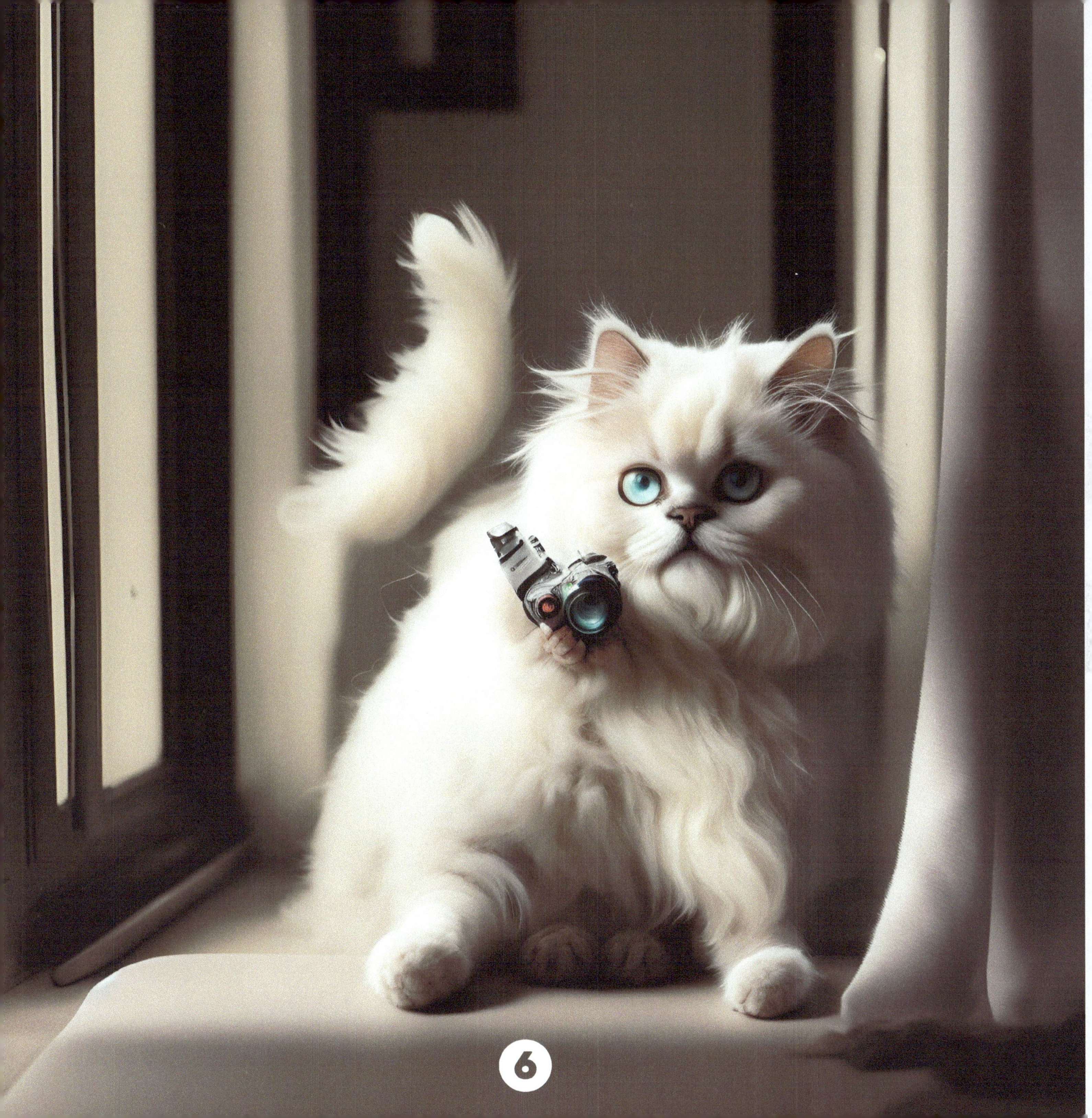

Chapter 4
Composition

Mounjaro learns about composition and how to frame a shot. She experiments with different angles, perspectives, and shapes to create a visually appealing photo.

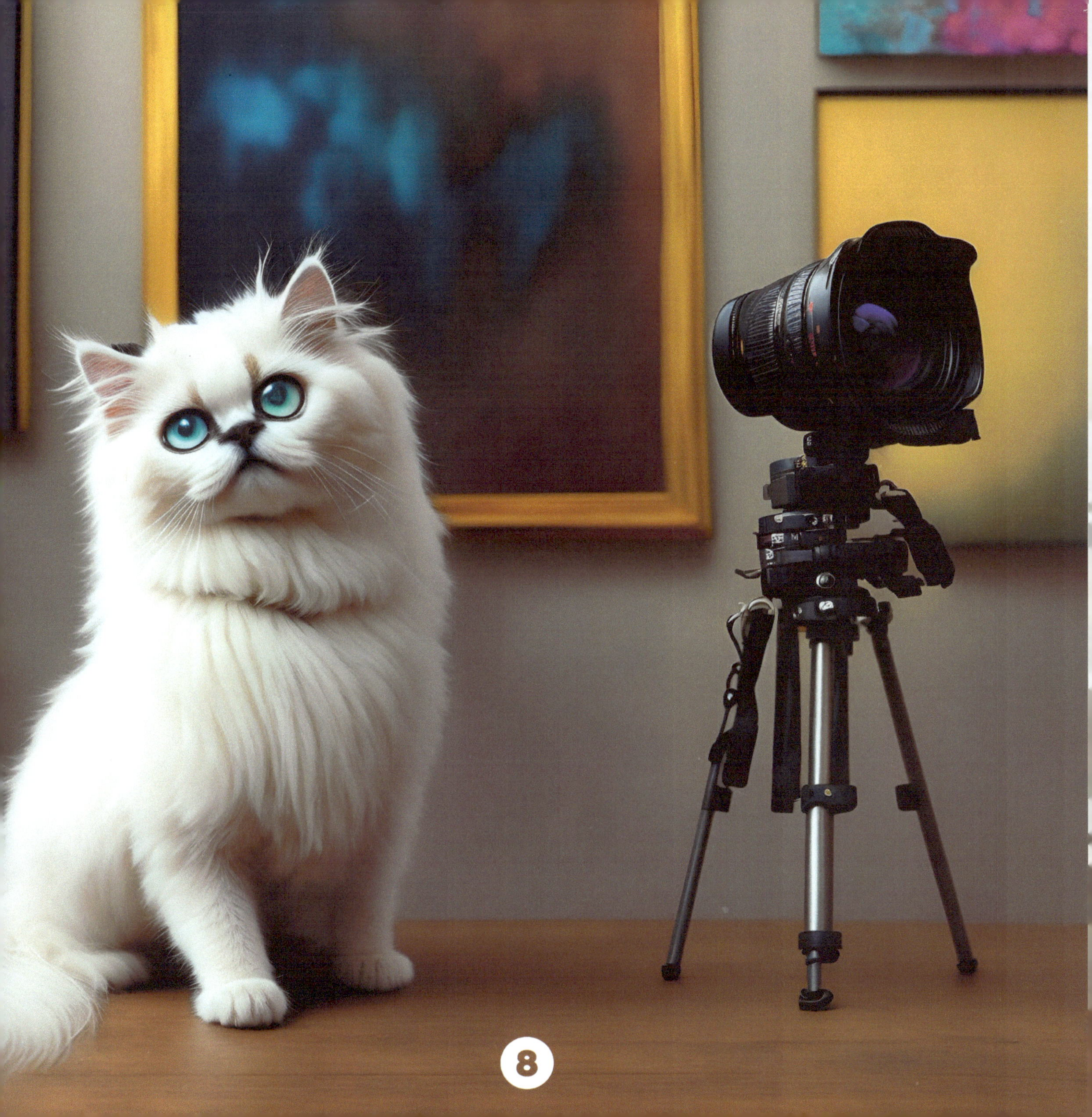

Chapter 5
Color

Mounjaro learns about color and how it can add depth and interest to a photo. She experiments with different color combinations and contrasts to create a stunning photograph.

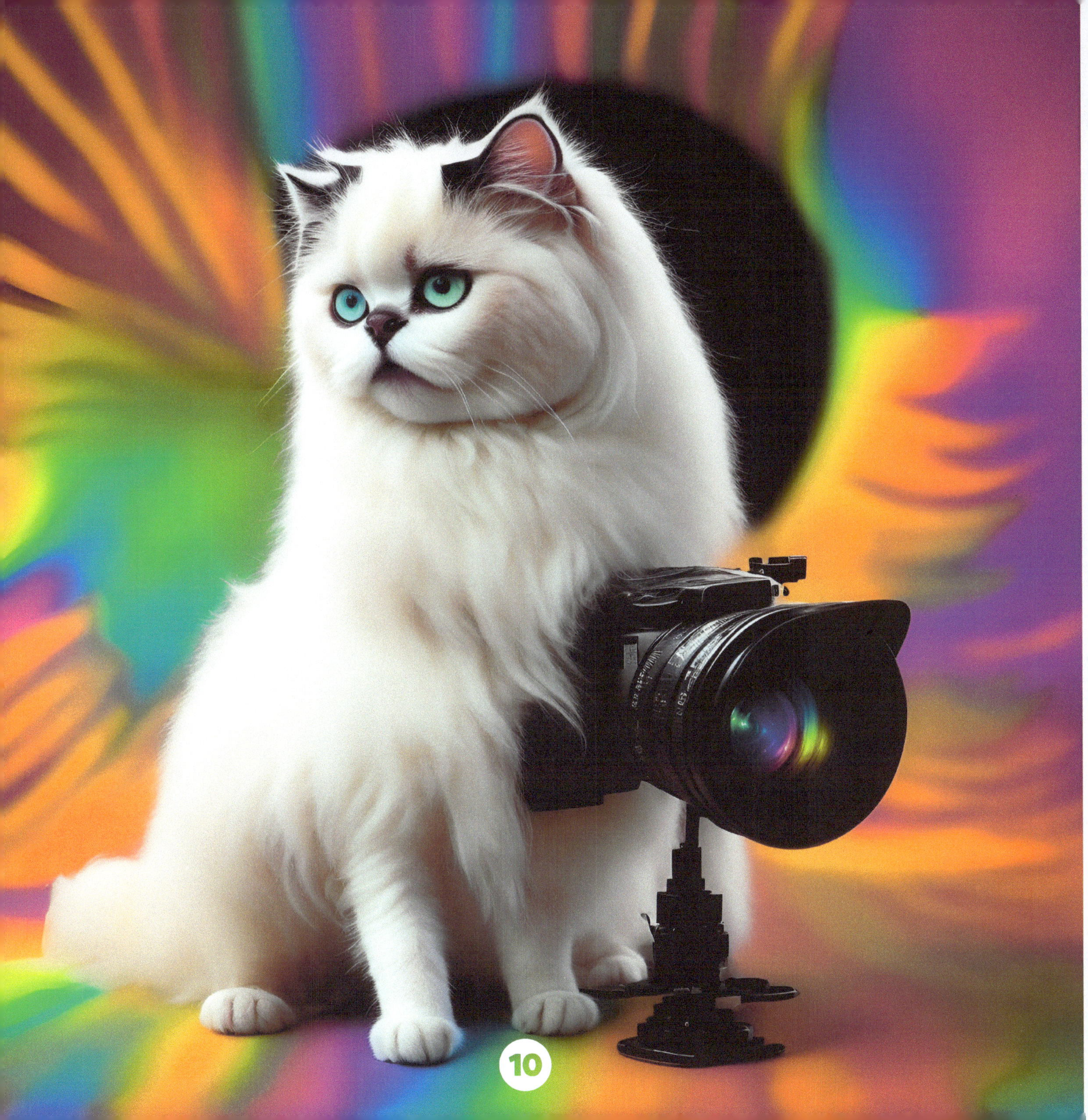

Chapter 6
Texture

Mounjaro discovers the beauty of texture and how it can add depth to a photo. She experiments with different textures, such as fur, grass, and water, to create a tactile photo.

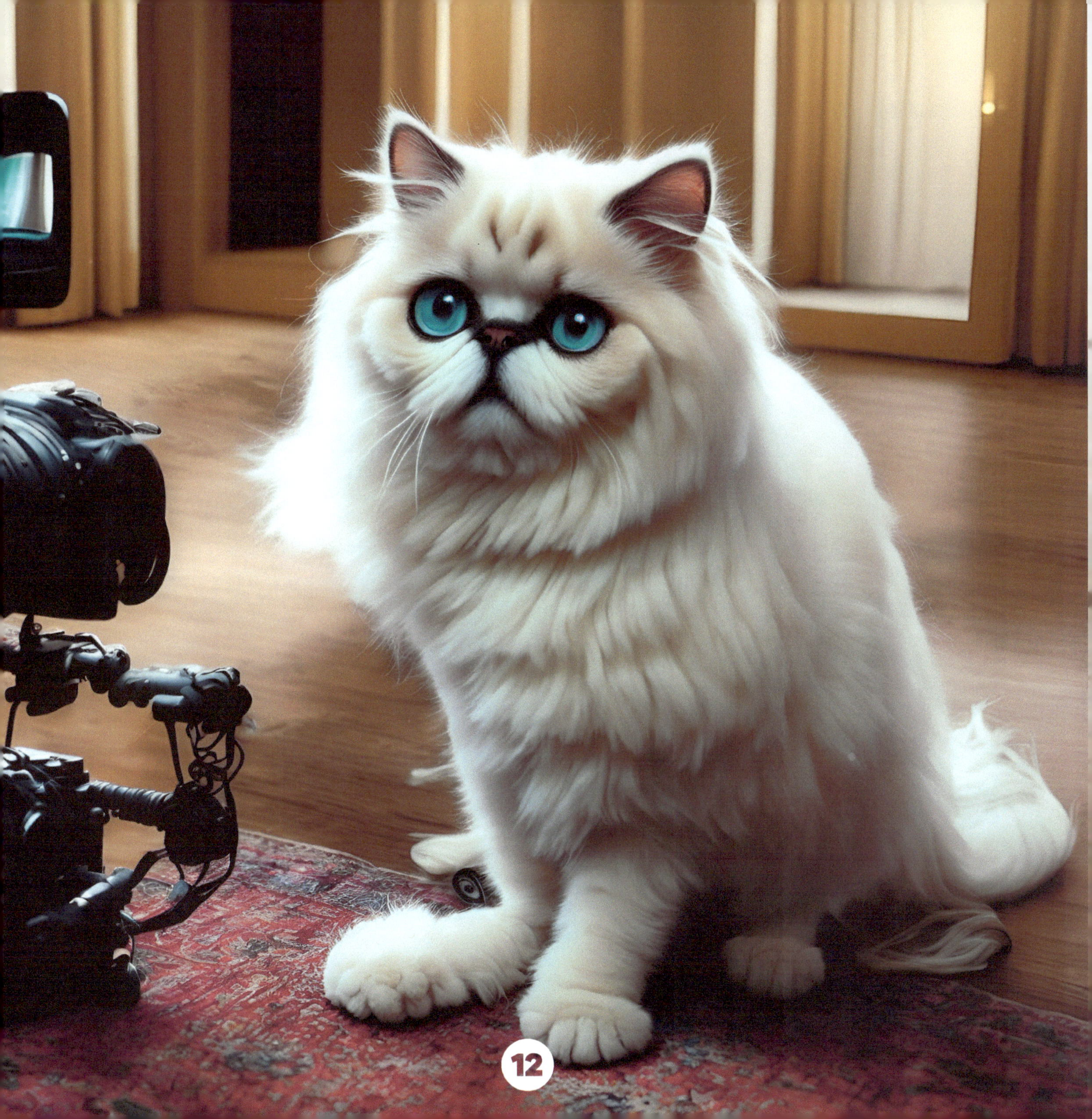

Chapter 7
Macro Photography

Mounjaro learns about macro photography and how to capture the small details of the world around her. She experiments with a macro lens to capture the intricate details of flowers, insects, and other small objects.

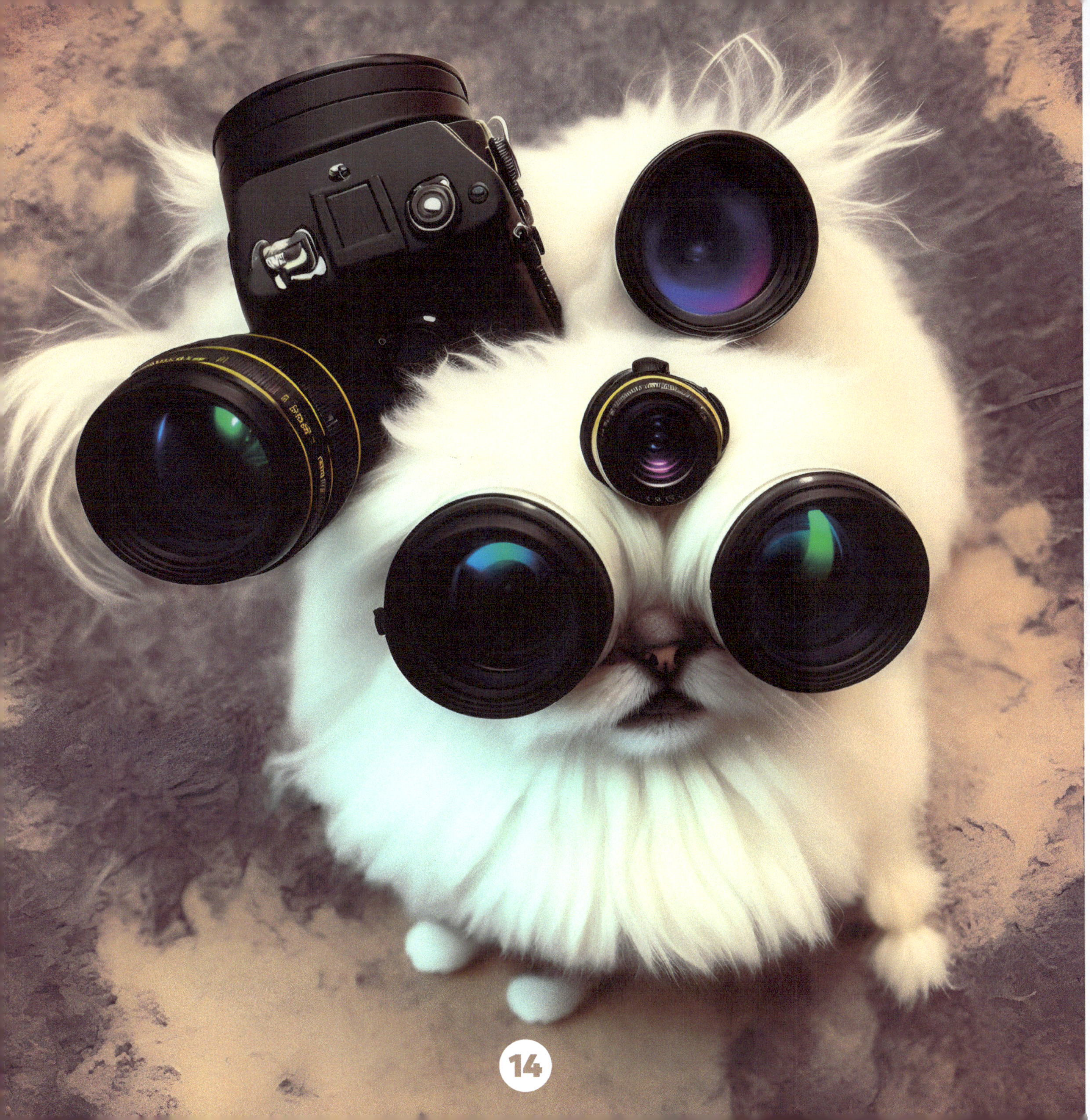

Mounjaro discovers portrait photography and how to capture the personality and emotions of her subjects. She experiments with different poses and expressions to create a meaningful portrait.

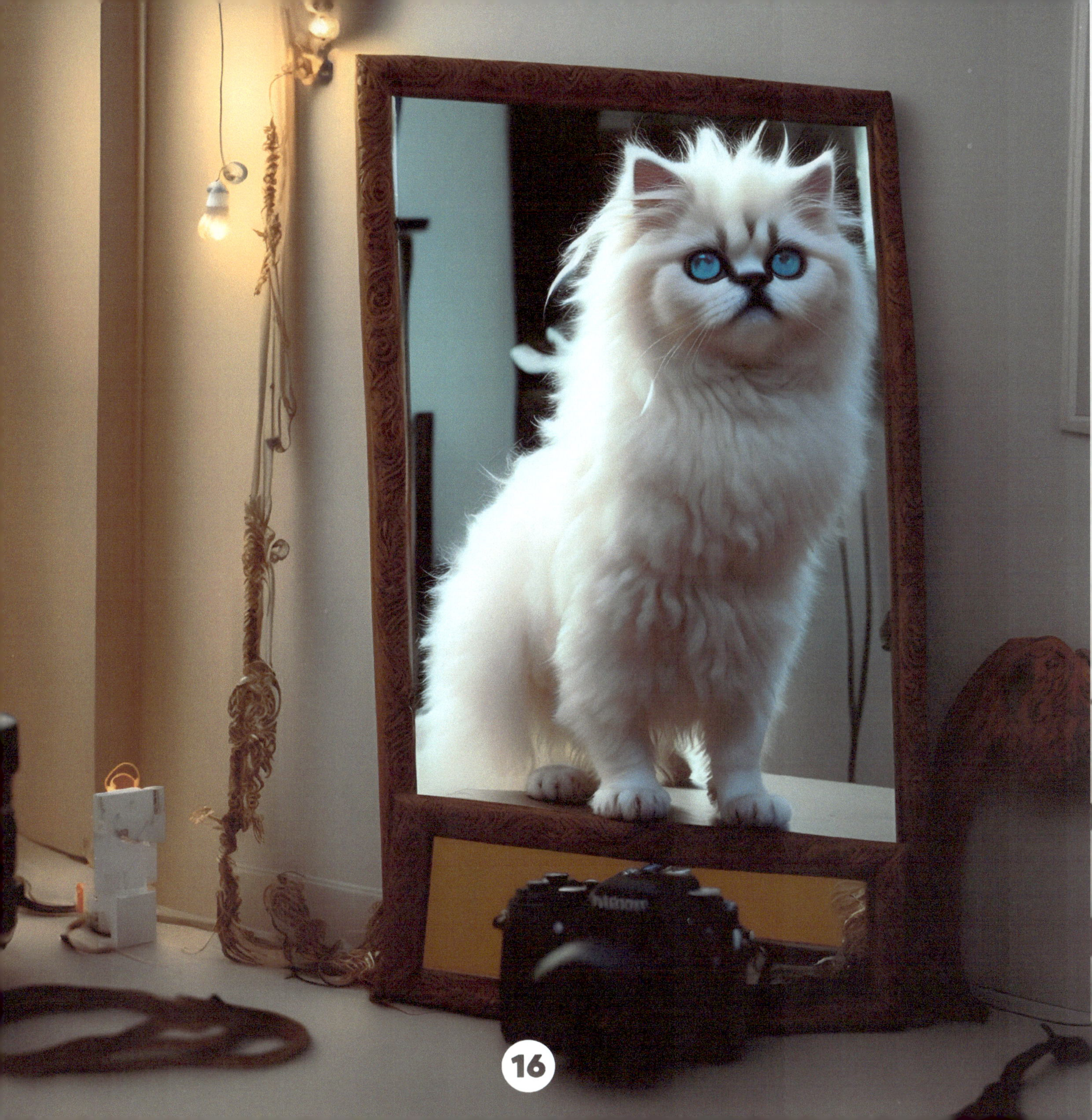

Chapter 9
Landscape Photography

Mounjaro discovers the beauty of nature and how to capture it in a photo. She experiments with different landscapes and weather conditions to create a stunning landscape photo.

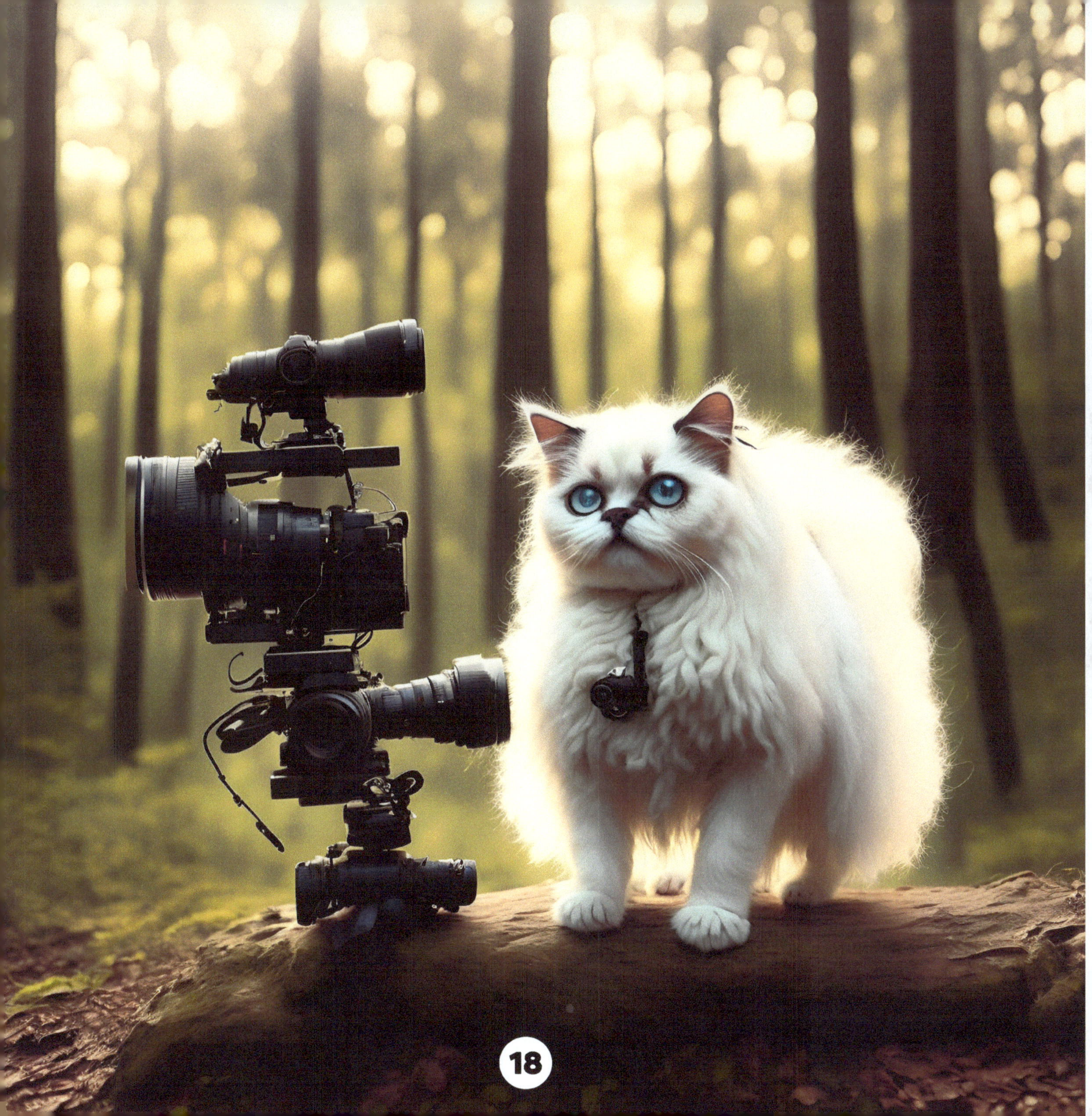

Chapter 10
Mindful Photography in Daily Life

Mounjaro realizes that photography is not just about taking pictures, but also about being mindful and present in the moment. She learns how to use photography as a tool to appreciate the small things in life and find beauty in everyday objects.

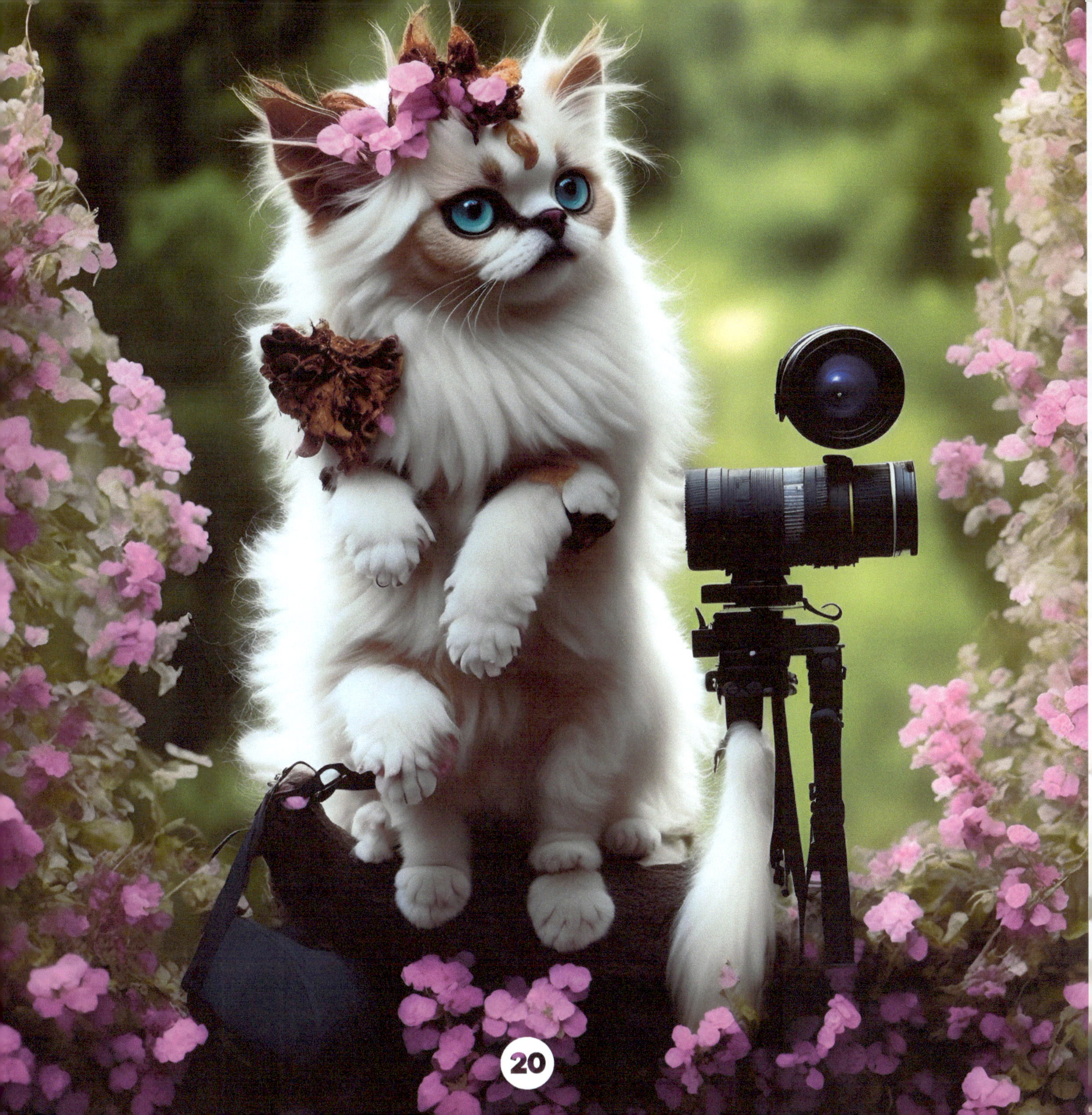

Teachers Guide

Chapter 1
You can introduce children to the concept of mindful photography and how it can help them appreciate the beauty around them.

Chapter 2
You can teach children about the basic functions of a camera and how they can adjust the settings to capture the perfect shot.

Chapter 3
You can teach children about the importance of light and shadow in photography and how they can use it to create different moods.

Chapter 4
You can teach children about the rule of thirds, leading lines, and other composition techniques to help them compose a great shot.

Chapter 5
You can teach children about the color wheel and how to use color to create a visually interesting photo.

Chapter 6
You can teach children about the importance of texture in photography and how to capture it in a photo.

Chapter 7
You can teach children about macro photography and how to capture the small details of the world around them.

Chapter 8
You can teach children about portrait photography and how to capture the essence of a person or animal in a photo.

Chapter 9
You can teach children about landscape photography and how to capture the beauty of nature in a photo.

Chapter 10
You can teach children how to apply mindful photography in their daily lives and how to use it as a tool to appreciate the world around them.

With these 10 chapters, children can learn about the different elements of mindful photography and how to apply them in their own photography. They can also follow Mounjaro's journey and discover the beauty of the world around them